Storms and Blessings

The true story of how one woman's faith helped her fight breast cancer

Sharon Griffiths

Storms and Blessings

Cover photograph taken by Neil Beer, www.neilbeer.com

Contact: sharongriffiths2010@hotmail.com

Published November 2010 by Life Publications, Merthyr Tydfil, South Wales, UK. Davidholdaway1@aol.com

Dedicated to my two beautiful daughters, who inspired me to never give up.

Acknowledgments

Thank you to my husband, Andrew who showed me love and commitment when the going got tough.

My girlies who showed such maturity and inspired me never to give up.

Thank you to my parents, Denis and Ronaldine who always inspire faith and strength and my brother Paul who flew all the way from Australia to "check up on me".

Thank you to my in-laws Tony and Anne, my sister-in-law Jackie, brother-in-law Steve, who showed much support and my sister-in-law, Maggie, who encouraged and advised me, after going through this experience herself.

Thank you to Helen, who showed true friendship and came on the journey with me.

Thank you to my friends from work who stayed in contact with me, every text, phone call and visit meant so much.

Thank you to all my family and friends who prayed me through the challenge.

Thank you to my surgeon, and my breast care nurse Ann who supported and encouraged me, she is not just a nurse but a friend.

Thank you 'bosom buddies', Fiona, Jackie and Sue for becoming lifelong friends as we faced our challenges together.

Thank you to all who made this book possible.

Contents

	Background of Author	7
Chapter One	My Roller Coaster Ride	9
Chapter Two	The Diagnosis	15
Chapter Three	Facing My Storm	23
Chapter Four	Fear Not	29
Chapter Five	The Consulting Room	35
Chapter Six	My New Look	39
Chapter Seven	Healing Rain	45
Chapter Eight	Chemo Blast	53
Chapter Nine	My Angel	59
Chapter Ten	Goodbye Hair	65
Chapter Eleven	Take A Break	71
Chapter Twelve	A Bridge To Blessings	77
Chapter Thirteen	The Big Op	83
Chapter Fourteen	Minus One	89
Chapter Fifteen	It Is Finished	95
	Epilogue	99

Storms and Blessings

Background of author

I was brought up as a minister's daughter, better known as a PK! (pastor's kid), so the church was like a second home to me. When we lived in Newcastle-upon-Tyne, it was even normal to spend Christmas Day in the church, feeding the Age Concern luncheon club members and those who were lonely. My mum, who has always put others first, would be in charge of a group of ladies, who would make Christmas dinner for a hall full of people. My brother, Paul, and I would take our new toys to the church and play. We learnt at an early age to respect and care for people. One Christmas when my dad was praying in his bedroom, my brother tip toed in and said, "This is God speaking, buy Paul a bike!" Even as children we knew the importance of God in our lives – he had his bike!

We were very proud of our parents, our dad was a respected man, and people put high expectations on me and my brother. People expected good behaviour and if we weren't, there'd be gasps or chuckles! I remember, as a child, talking to my friends in one of the meetings and a new lady was sitting in front of me. In the middle of the service she turned around and said, "Where is your mother?" I pointed to a lady I didn't know and disappeared to the toilet. I didn't like to tell her my dad was the man on the platform!

People would often ask me for information if they missed the church notices. This wasn't always a good idea because once

I told someone the wrong person had died! I had to ring them up and apologise! There were many amusing moments but most importantly I began to have encounters with God and feel the Holy Spirit in meetings.

As a child and throughout my life I've been introduced to people with great faith. I was born with the condition of clicking hips. My parents were told I would have to have an operation and be in plaster for quite a while. Their first reaction was to pray that God would touch and heal me. Their prayers were answered; I was healed as a baby. I didn't have to have an operation. My childhood memories include being in meetings where a person getting healed was very normal. My dad prayed for a little boy who had a critical deteriorating illness and God healed him, the doctors were amazed and admitted it was a miracle. Blind eyes were opened and other miracles happened. Seeing this as a young child increases your faith without any doubts. It was the firm foundation of my faith in God.

I became a qualified primary school teacher and have taught for sixteen years. I met my husband in Swansea and we have two beautiful daughters and a dog! Little did we know that I would end up having to fight the biggest challenge of my life at thirty eight-years-old – breast cancer. I pray the journal of my story will be of help and encouragement to anyone facing cancer or if you know someone who is. I made jottings of my one year's experience and recorded it to share. A journey of tears and laughter, storms and blessings.

1

My Roller Coaster Ride

I tucked my youngest girl, Shona, in bed and whispered, "Goodnight". My arm brushed against my left breast – there was a lump on the side. I wasn't alarmed as I'd had a mammogram three years previously and it was clear, only cysts detected. I naturally thought that this was the same.

I worked as a full time primary teacher so decided I would have it checked in the next holiday. Weeks went by and soon it was the wonderful break I had been looking forward to. I had been feeling run down and exhausted. My under active thyroid had been playing up so I blamed all my unwell feelings on this. My thyroid got the blame for many of my weak moments as my family and friends would verify!

The second week of the holidays I remembered I should book the appointment but nearly didn't, as I felt I didn't want to be a burden to the doctor again – I'd recently had pain in my side which needed blood tests and an ovarian scan.

The appointment was made! The doctor examined me and decided that on this examination there was nothing to worry about as the lump was mobile. She booked a mammogram, just in case. I didn't even think of the lump again until the hospital appointment. My mum and I went as my husband, Andrew, was teaching, none of us aware of what we were about to experience.

I sat in the waiting area after my mammogram, watching the other ladies coming out smiling after their results – then it was my turn. Two nurses entered the room smiling, a doctor entered saying they were going to look more closely at the lump on my left side. Another doctor entered the room followed by a consultant. My stomach began to turn; I felt the seriousness of all the faces around me although they were being very reassuring. The doctor did an ultra sound scan; again my right side had cysts but my left they wanted to investigate. One of them began to draw a circle around the lump. They explained they wanted to take three biopsies and a Fine Needle Aspirate sample from the lymph gland.

I knew this was serious. I prayed, "Oh, God just help me not to faint!" I closed my eyes, what was happening? I wanted to walk out like the other ladies smiling and go back to work. But that wasn't meant to be. The nurse put her arm around me and asked if I wanted my mother in the room when the consultant talked to me. I felt I couldn't take in anything he was about to say. I tried to smile at mum when I saw her brave, concerned face.

He began to say I was young, and what they had found had the "appearance of something concerning". That's all I could remember. The nurse stroked my arm and I felt sick and shocked. Whenever I had thought about death before I would feel anxious, even though I believe I am going to heaven. God gave me an inner peace that I will always remember at that crucial moment, even though the doctor hadn't mentioned death. He chose his words very carefully but I felt I was being prepared for bad news. There was a whole bank holiday weekend extra to wait. My results appointment was in eight days time. How was I going to wait that long? It seemed like forever. Mum and I just looked at each other. I kept repeating, "I can't believe it, I can't believe it."

Mum phoned my work to say I wouldn't be back that afternoon. I thank God for my boss, who said I could stay off work until the results were through. She'd heard my mother's concern. I went into shock. I found it hard to swallow, my brain felt as if it was exploding. I couldn't cry. I'm usually emotional, but I just couldn't cry. I drove straight home, Andrew was there, he tried to comfort me and felt we should just wait for the official results. Mum phoned my dad to come and pick her up. My dad put his arm around me and that is when the tears started. He said, "Just pray for God's presence to be around you." Then the exhausted feeling came over me and I said I just needed to sleep. Mum and dad went home and I went to bed.

As soon as my head hit the pillow my imagination started working. What if I am going to die? What about my lovely children and husband? What if it has spread? What if they only give me months to live? What will I tell my girls? "Oh, Lord," I prayed, "just help me". I struggled for an hour with these thoughts going through my head. I felt as if I was burying myself. Suddenly I sensed God reminding me of His greatness. He said, "You believe in me so why struggle? You believe I am a healing God so why lie down and become overwhelmed with these thoughts?" I suddenly jumped out of bed; I wasn't going to let these negative thoughts get the better of me. "Yes Lord, you are right, I am not going to lie down and give in to this. We are going to fight it together – You and me."

That was the start of a very emotional roller coaster week. I hadn't been told I had breast cancer, but felt as if I had. I was in shock for two days. I found it hard to swallow; my mouth was dry, food would stick in my throat, I could only drink. I prayed over the lump every day that God would protect me. One minute you can't believe and don't want to believe that this could happen. The next minute you are building yourself up to face reality. My husband, family and friends were very encouraging and I thank them for that. I remember praying one night and saying to God, "I am choosing life God, I am choosing life." A warmth came around me and I felt as if my face was being cupped in His hands. I sensed a smiling face and God whispered to me, "Yes, my child." This was an amazing experience; I had such peace knowing He was going to help me.

My Roller Coaster Ride

I had to prepare my young girls who were ten and six years old that I may have to go into hospital. I didn't want them to have a terrible shock next week, if the diagnosis was cancer. I spoke to Chloe, my eldest first. I explained I had a lump in my breast and the doctor had done tests to see if I had to have it taken away or not. I may have to have an operation. As expected she was upset, we cried together and then laughed at how emotional we were. I told her not to worry and she made me promise to tell her everything when I knew more. I made that promise and kept it. Shona said she just didn't want me to go into hospital. I said I may not have to and not to worry.

My faith this week began to rise; I began to gain a strength that only God can give. I felt as if I was holding on to all that I believed in, with two hands! I believe He was preparing me for what lay ahead. I was given a chapter from the Bible to read from a friend that would be of encouragement – Psalm 121 which starts by saying, *"I will lift up my eyes to the hills – where does my help come from? My help comes from the Lord, the Maker of heaven and earth..."* That was the beginning of many verses that would uphold me during this time.

As I began to read the Bible every verse seemed to be preparing me for a battle that lay ahead and I hadn't even had the results yet! I sneaked a look at my daily Bible readings for the date I was getting my results, hoping it would be inspirational but when I looked it said to put on the armour of God! Oh, no I thought, this doesn't look good. Then my dad phoned me and said he had a verse of scripture for me Proverbs 3:5,6, *"Trust in the Lord with all your heart and lean not on your own understanding. In all your ways acknowledge Him and He will make your paths straight."*

That was when I really felt I knew what lay ahead – I had a battle to face but in the end it was going to be ok. Slowly, very slowly, the day approached for the results. At last it was Tuesday...

2

The Diagnosis

Tuesday eventually arrived; a strange feeling took over me of relief and dread. How on earth was I going to wait till 3.30pm? My close friend, Helen invited me over for coffee. It was great until I went to the bathroom and came out crying at 12pm! We hugged each other and she prayed for God to help me on the journey ahead. It was a strange feeling of knowing what the doctor was going to say but not accepting it until he did.

My husband and I braved ourselves as we travelled to the hospital only to learn that the consultant was running an hour late! Eventually the lady who was sitting anxiously in the waiting room with me went in and came out in five minutes smiling. Ok, I thought, here I go Lord, please help me. I had prayed that I wouldn't have breast cancer but if I had please, please Lord let them tell me it is treatable.

Storms and Blessings

We were called into a consulting room; the nurse greeted us with a lovely smile. Did this mean she had good news? My stomach turned as I saw the consultant come in, the memories of last week came flooding back. Andrew and I sat on the lovely leather settee holding each others' hand so tight. The consultant smiled tenderly and reminded me of the intense circumstances we had met under the week before. He carried on to say that the lump had an appearance of something concerning and that the concern was correct. I had breast cancer and it had also gone to the lymph gland where they had taken the sample. I took a deep breath; he stopped talking for a minute while Andrew and I just stared in shock at the reality of what we had just heard. Did that mean the end – there was no hope?

The nurse went to get me some water, once again I couldn't cry but this time it was Andrew's turn. The emotion of the moment hit him; he was trying to be so strong for me. Tears welled and flowed but he kept asking if I was ok. The consultant carried on to say it was treatable with chemotherapy and radiotherapy. Thank you Lord – that was an answer to prayer. He wanted to do a lumpectomy and remove all my lymph glands from under my left arm. If he found that not all the cancer was removed from my breast in the first operation I would have to be operated on again and again until it was. The surrounding area had to be cancer free. The other option was a mastectomy, which he didn't think was needed. My first reaction was for him to remove the breast so I was definitely cancer free. He advised me that this wasn't necessary and he was happy to proceed with the lumpectomy. He was giving us time to decide on which operation we wanted. He stressed that I was young and he wanted to keep my cleavage. At this point both Andrew and I laughed and said there wasn't much of a cleavage to keep!

The consultant said he wanted me to have a CT scan and bone scan before the operation. My first thought was, "Oh no, he thinks it has spread already." I felt physically sick. He proceeded to tell me that this was procedure – but that didn't help! He said he had to have base scans to know what treatment was best for me. Every twinge I had felt in the last month came into my head – could it have been a sign of cancer?

After the consultant had gone the breast care nurse stayed with us, calming all anxieties. She was such a wonderful lady, a lady who would become a special friend and great strength when I needed advice and encouragement, she put me at rest immediately. She explained that she would be the nurse to change my dressings on the ward after the operation; she would be with me through the treatment and at the end of the phone if ever we needed her. The only thing she asked of us was at the end of all this we would send her a postcard from our holiday! The thought of this immediately filled us with hope.

I had many questions to ask her, two of which were "Am I going to die?" and, "Am I going to see my children grow up?" My children were the trigger that made my emotions go haywire! She put her arm around me and said, "You will see them graduate and grow up." At this point I burst into tears.

Andrew and I just sat and cried for a few minutes but she was so reassuring, she was God sent.

How was I going to tell my girls? I asked her advice and she said to tell them I had a nasty lump that had to be removed. She gave me a wonderful story book called *Mummy's Lump* and information about the type of cancer I had – Grade 2 invasive duct cancer.

First I phoned my parents, they must have been sitting on the phone because they answered immediately! I prayed in my head that God would protect them. My dad was still recovering from open heart surgery he had two years previously in Australia. I didn't want him to be ill because of me. Their faith in God through every situation is inspirational. I heard dad's voice, "Well, what did they say love?" I could only reply, "Dad, I've got it and it's gone to my lymph glands but don't worry it's treatable." I couldn't talk any more I was crying too much. Andrew dropped me off at their house to explain everything and answer any questions they had. Dad was already waiting at the door, while mum was looking through the window anxiously. I cried but not for long, I had a strange feeling of relief because it was treatable. My mum said she had felt this relief as well as soon as she had heard the news that it was treatable. I explained everything and answered the questions they had.

I had already sent a text to my in-laws to tell them. We had agreed to communicate like this because they were looking after the girls for me. This way I could talk to the girls first and explain the situation when I was ready.

The Diagnosis

Next hurdle was to phone work. I couldn't believe what I was saying; "I have breast cancer." I found it very emotional telling people and hearing their emotional response upset me. I didn't want people to feel sad because of me, I felt guilty for upsetting people. I came to realise it was easier for others to tell people instead of me. But as someone once told me, God saves all the tears you've cried as a rainfall of blessing for later.

Next were my girls – they came home, I took a big breath! I had imagined once what it would be like to have to tell them something serious like this and I would cry at the thought of it. But when I actually had to do it an overwhelming strength came over me. I was determined they would understand the situation and not worry. Chloe's immediate question as she walked through the door was, "Do you have to go to hospital?" I nodded and said, "Yes, I'll tell you all about it." The children sat on the settee; I knelt in between them on the floor so I could see their faces. I took a deep breath and started, "I have been to the doctors today and he says I have to go to hospital. I've got a nasty lump in my boob and he wants to take it away. If he doesn't I will get very ill." The girls were crying. Shona didn't want me to spend any time away from home. "Please mum," she said, "Don't go into hospital." I replied, "I have to go so I can get better. You want mummy to get better don't you?" "Yes," she replied through her whimpers. Chloe wanted to know about her birthday party which had been arranged. Andrew and I had planned to take two cars of children to Cardiff. I told her that if she wanted me to be part of the birthday we had to bring her party forward or Auntie Jackie would be home from Malawi and she could drive the second car. She decided to keep her party on the same date as arranged. I was so proud of them. I told Chloe if she wanted to ask more questions we would talk later. She was happy with this as she always likes her one to one moments. The three of us had a family cuddle, the girls were still crying then Chloe turned to Shona and said, "At least we have each other Shona, we will be there for each other." It was then I began to fill up as we just hugged each other. I changed the subject and we began to try and make Shona laugh! It didn't take long and soon she was asleep.

Chloe was waiting for our chat, the first question was... "Are you going to die?" other questions were, "What is the lump called?" "Can I catch it if you kiss or hug me?" "Are you going to lose all your hair?" She was very sensible in all the questions she asked and I answered every one honestly. I explained that the lump they had found was called breast cancer. We talked about the chemotherapy and radiotherapy. I wasn't going to explain so much so quickly but with each question she asked she wanted to know the honest answers. We read the book together *Mummy's Lump*. I hugged her very tightly and told her to make me a promise. I said if ever she needed someone to talk to, she must talk. She must never hold onto anything that is worrying her and let it upset her. She could pray about it, talk to family or friends, I didn't mind, just as long as she was happy. She asked if she was allowed to tell her friends, I said of course, I would never want her to keep something like this a secret because she had to have friends to support her as well.

The Diagnosis

Slowly the news started to spread. My friend said there was a feeling of shock in the church on the first Sunday. I had attended this church since eleven years of age when my father became the minister. I had asked our present minister to pray for me, that way, once again, it saved me from having to tell people. Friends couldn't believe what they were hearing. I am so grateful to my family and friends for all their support and concern during these initial stages of my diagnosis. I had many texts, phone calls, flowers, cards, visits and most importantly I had many who said they would pray for me. I had people praying for me in England, Ireland, Scotland and Wales, Africa, Australia, New Zealand, America and more! All around the world! How encouraging was this! I thought, "God you are going to have to help me through this, because you are going to get tired of hearing my name up there!"

You go through a stage of asking yourself many questions about how you may have "caught" this. Have I had too many take-aways? Was I really eating a healthy diet? Did I exercise enough? Or was it that I just stood too close to the microwave when it was on? It seems so ridiculous! One of my first experiments was to try goat's milk because I had heard dairy products weren't too good for you. I put the goat's milk on my crunchy nut cornflakes; I sat down with a familiar smell of a farm visit going up my nostrils! I put one spoonful in my mouth and can only say it was like sucking a pair of udders! That was my first and last attempt at goat's milk.

My faith at this time went into overdrive; one example of this was when Chloe was very concerned about her homework that had been very crumpled up in her bag. I told her to put it under her Bible and pray for God to straighten it by the morning! She laughed and said, "Oh, mum you don't have to pray for everything!"

During this tense week I found it difficult to sleep so I asked the doctor if she could suggest something to help me relax. She gave me mild sleeping tablets. I had never taken sleeping pills before, so I thought I would take one at 8pm and by 10pm I would be feeling relaxed! A friend phoned just after I'd taken the tablet so I sat talking for half an hour before the doorbell rang. I went to stand and my knees buckled! I was holding onto everything to get to the hallway. I answered the door to one of the leaders of our youth group in a drunken state! I usually ran the club with her and she needed the register. We laughed as I held onto the banister to try and walk upstairs to get it. Coming down was even more hysterical!

3

Facing My Storm

I had to have two scans before going into hospital – a CT scan and bone scan, to make sure it hadn't gone anywhere else. These were times of really holding on to my faith and praying that the cancer was only contained in the areas we knew of. My daily Bible readings had been such strength to me. The night before my CT scan I opened my daily reading and it said, *"Fear not, for I am with you..."* Isaiah 41:10. I prayed earnestly and said to God, "I am terrified of the results, oh God, please let them be clear." I opened my Bible and there was Joshua 1:9, *"Be strong and courageous. Do not be terrified; do not be discouraged, for the Lord your God will be with you wherever you go."* Wow! What a direct answer to prayer. It was times like these I knew I wasn't doing it in my own strength but God was with me every step of the way.

The morning came of my CT scan and I had to drink my potions – 500ml of water with the added flavouring two hours before then one litre of water one hour before, with the added flavourings. I added so much cordial I think I curdled my stomach! It wasn't the most lady like of days! My parents picked me up as Chloe had to go for an X-ray on the same day. Mum and I laughed because the sign directly in front of the seats in the waiting area read, "Toilet down corridor on left!" Whilst waiting, we knew who was having a scan because we all took it in turns to run down the corridor!

The same day as my scan my minister came to visit and have a light lunch with us. I had to excuse myself three times because of the side effects of the scan! Fortunately, he continued talking to my husband so I don't think he noticed and if he did, he's got a good sense of humour anyway. Whilst he prayed for me, I prayed I wouldn't embarrass myself with unladylike sounds!

When you are waiting for the results you tend to think of all the aches and pains you have had in the last six months and start to question the diagnosis given by the doctors at that time. Was it really cancer after all? I thank God that our prayers for a clear CT scan came with much relief. I was over the moon. I felt as if a heavy burden had been lifted from my shoulders. When the nurse gave me the results she laughed, my screams of delight could be heard by all the nurses in the office. She encouraged me and said the bone scan was just procedure now.

The bone scan – that was an experience. I am not the greatest and bravest of people, so when they told me I would be radio active for 24 hours after the injection, I thought this can't be good! But surprisingly it wasn't as bad as I thought. I had to be injected with the radio active ingredients two hours before the scan. We had permission to go home during the waiting time. I told Andrew if we got romantic in the night he would glow in the dark! On our return to the hospital we passed a couple who commented that they had gone really hot as they passed me! Andrew and I laughed, the injection had worked! Once more I thank God that the results of this scan came back clear as well.

Preparations had to be made for my stay in hospital. First on my list was a full supportive bra that the nurse had recommended for me to buy. It would act like a supportive bandage. When I was asking the assistants in the shop for advice because I was going in for an operation, each one gave me the same look. They would firstly smile, then look straight at my breasts and give me a knowing look and nod. I know what they thought – they thought I was going in for enlargements! Mum and I did laugh over this.

Through my experience so far I felt strongly that I should make a journal, so much had happened in such a short time. I prayed that my experience would be an encouragement, a blessing to someone, even a practical helping guide. I didn't tell anyone about my thoughts initially but it was to be confirmed by my mother-in-law. She phoned me one morning and said she had been praying for me, she had e-mailed me what she felt the Lord was telling me. This was the e-mail:

> *As I was praying for you last night I felt the*
> *Lord speak to me and to tell you that you must*

keep a journal. Not just what is happening to you physically but your thoughts and feelings. Not necessarily a daily "diary" but what you are experiencing and what the Lord will be saying to you and showing you. I also felt that although there will be difficult times **everything will be fine.** *I was reminded of Joseph in my daily reading that although he went through such a hard time God brought good out of the bad situation.*

Wow! Yet another experience to confirm to me that God is in control and knows everything! This was a direct confirmation about what I had been feeling since the beginning. I told my friend Helen about it and before I knew it she was presenting me with a little gift. I opened it and there was my journal with the inscription on the front "Everything will be alright." When I opened it she had written:

God has already written it and it is finished! This chapter is about to start but will end...in victory!

After reading this I burst into tears and felt so privileged to be so encouraged. Every day I prayed for strength to get through the day, some days I felt stronger than others. I remember the Sunday before my operation was a particularly weak day! I felt as if all my strength had gone, I was emotional...until I read my daily reading. The title was, "Two lessons to learn only in life's storms." *"Why are you so fearful?"* Mark 4:40.

It reminded me that in the gospel of Mark we read,

"Jesus said to them, 'Let us cross over to the other side'... And a great storm arose, and the waves beat into the boat, so that it was already filling. But He was in the stern, asleep on a pillow. And they awoke Him and said to Him, 'Teacher, do you not care that we are perishing?' Then He arose and rebuked the wind, and said to the sea, 'Peace be still!' And the wind ceased and there was a great calm. But He said to them, 'Why are you so fearful? How is it that you have no faith?' And they said to one another, 'Who can this be, that even the wind and the sea obey Him!'"

Mark 4:35-41

The reading went on to say the two lessons you learn only when you face life's storms are:

1. *You must trust what God has told you.* What has God promised you? Standing on that won't keep you from being scared or soaked, but it'll keep you from sinking.

2. *You must remind yourself who's in the boat with you.* If the Lord can calm a storm, He can prevent one. So when He permits you to go through storms it's to show you that you don't have a problem He can't solve; that you may be powerless in the situation but He's not; and that through this experience you'll

come to know Him in a way you have never known Him before. So learn these lessons well and come out stronger on the other side.

I lay on my bed smiling, isn't God amazing? Just when I needed another boost I got one! A friend sent me a Keith and Kristyn Getty CD, words from one particular song really meant so much to me and it really became my prayer,

> *"Jesus, draw me ever nearer as I labour through the storm; You have called me to this passage, and I'll follow, though I'm worn. May this journey bring a blessing, may I rise on wings of faith; and at the end of my heart's testing, with your likeness let me wake. Jesus guide me through the tempest, keep my spirit staid and sure; when the midnight meets the morning, let me love You even more. Let the treasures of the trial form within me as I go – and at the end of this long passage, let me leave them at your throne."*

4

Fear Not

The day of the operation soon arrived. The nurse had given me a list of items to take in to hospital which helped greatly. I will list them in case they are of help to someone – mobile phone, wet wipes, open front pyjamas or nightie with short sleeves (pjs best as you only have to reveal one part of your body in examinations!), 100 per cent cotton pants for theatre, soft supportive bra (no underwire), bed socks (optional), hobbies – books, i-pod (I found an i-pod fantastic), toiletries, slippers, dressing gown, towels. I took in photos of my girls and also my own pillow.

My main prayer before going into hospital was that there would be someone I could relate to, who was a similar age to me. I walked into the ward room and there were two lovely ladies waiting by their beds. Then in walked a lady one year younger than myself, who was having exactly the same op as me, she had two children, similar ages to mine. God is even interested in the small things. The three ladies I met that day ended up being very good friends, we supported each other through every stage. I call them my "bosom buddies."

This was to be a major operation; they said it would take about one and half hours to remove all my lymph glands from under my arm and a lumpectomy of the breast. I was to have two drains, one of which would be removed in hospital; the other was to stay in for approximately a week. I had all the pre operation tests, everything was fine. They gave me the option of a premed, I took it. I wanted everything they could give me! The night before the operation I was listening to the song *How Great is our God* and I opened my Bible which said, *"Fear not for I am with you,"* Isaiah 41:10. I was being encouraged spiritually and physically by people around me. My room mates and the nurses were fantastic. When you are with people going through the same circumstances as yourself you can make light of certain situations, which helped. I would say that this is an extremely important part of the journey – making friends with those who are going through the same as yourself.

I had my premed – what an experience! It was a great experience to feel so relaxed. I was wheeled down to the operating theatre where I saw my surgeon – the tears started flowing. I wasn't expecting it, but they did. The poor man only said hello to me. He rubbed my arm and left the nurse to talk with me! I soon settled and was out of it. I came around to see mum, dad and Andrew around my bed back on the ward. But apparently that wasn't the beginning of me coming around! My friend in the next bed said I came into the room, waving to everyone like the Queen. I looked at her and asked if she still had her nipple! She had just come back from theatre and said she wasn't sure. She had to ask someone to check! I apologised, I just couldn't remember saying it, and we had such a laugh over it. Apparently, my mum was by my bed and I kept repeating that I was in a lovely place!

After I had spoken to mum and dad, they left, so that Andrew and I could have time together. I kept telling Andrew he was gorgeous and I wanted him to come into bed for cuddles! I remember he kept repeating he couldn't because we were in hospital. I said it didn't matter and I told him I would move up so he had space to get into bed! I was persistent apparently and he kept saying no and laughing. First time ever he's turned me down! He had been very concerned that I wouldn't come around after the anaesthetic, so he was feeling very relieved.

My daily reading for my operation day was "God is protecting you." It went on to ask – "Would you protect your own child from harm? Multiply that by infinity and you'll understand how much God cares for you." This was another dose of encouragement. Friends and family were so good to me at this time; I had so many text messages, gifts, poems, flowers, cards and messages of support. I will always be grateful for this.

One of the ladies I was sharing a room with was a brilliant snorer! We had a few sleepless nights, so a couple of us would escape to the visitors lounge at two in the morning to have a cup of tea with the night staff. It was an experience! My breast care nurse came to the ward to check me and remove the initial bandages. It was so wonderful to see a familiar face, someone you can trust and answer any questions and put your mind at ease. They were pleased with how the operation had gone, I was just glad it was over.

When it was time to go home, I believed I had made lifelong friends. We came from different backgrounds, one was an occupational therapist, one was a nurse, one had just finished working in a dry cleaners and I was the teacher. We all had a story to tell, little did I realise at this stage what a regular support these friends would be. It is at times like these you realise that no matter what your background, we were in the same boat and needed the same reassurances and encouragement.

It was only when I got home that I realised how much energy the operation had taken away. I struggled to get up the stairs. My children were so excited to have me home but I felt rotten. Apparently, it was because I had a bad reaction to the anti inflammatory tablets they had given me. I had terrible stomach cramps and a feeling of going to faint for many hours. My girls had been to Cardiff for my eldest daughter's birthday party, as planned. I tried my best to be enthusiastic but could hardly even smile. I felt terrible and it worried them to see me so ill. They all sat on the bed to tell me about the party and I remember my youngest daughter falling backwards off the end of the bed and I couldn't even react to save her as I watched it happening. Fortunately, my dad and sister-in-law were on hand to help with the girls. The girls got quite upset to see me like this and they kept repeating that I should have stayed in hospital! But after a rough night I started to feel more human again, much to everyone's relief.

One of my friends, who I had met in hospital, decided we should meet up at one of the local relaxation classes in the cancer centre at the hospital. We were encouraged to get involved in sessions that were being held there. I was a bit apprehensive, we both still had our drains in and my arm movement was very limited. Well, we arrived slightly late, after having a chat outside. It was so great to see her again. When we walked in it was so quiet and everyone was so focused and serious. The instructor welcomed us and we had to find a space. She encouraged us all to lift our arms above our heads and bring them down in front of us, breathing slowly. I began to have the giggles as I could only do it with one arm! She tip toed behind me and tried to lift the other arm up. I think she thought I was trying to be funny! I yelped that I had a drain in. I hadn't been there for long and already I had shattered the quietness of the room!

At one time in the session we had to lie on the floor, she encouraged us to imagine walking along a lovely beach, with the sun shining. This made me remember the holiday we had just cancelled because of this! Everyone around me seemed really into it and it must have been working for them. I tried not to giggle too much but sometimes when you shouldn't laugh is the time you want to even more! During the session, she encouraged us to think about peace. She said she would ring a bell after every minute for five minutes. I sat there with my eyes closed thinking, "You know what? I believe in a God who can give you peace instantly if you ask Him, so I think

I'll keep to that." In this time I prayed that God would help me in the weeks that were to come and I had peace and reassurance that He was with me. They were lovely people in the session but it just wasn't for me.

5

The Consulting Room

I stayed in close contact with one of the ladies I met in the hospital through text and phone calls. The next time we met up was the day of our operation results. My stomach turned as I walked into the breast care building. The last time I had been there was the day of my diagnosis. As I walked in she was just coming out after seeing the consultant, she didn't look happy. We gave each other a huge hug. It was then she told me that they hadn't been able to remove all the cancer and she had to have another operation. I was gutted for her. But first the family wanted to go on the holiday they had booked a while ago, to America! She was given the ok to go and the operation would take place when she returned. She had more courage than me because I would have been too nervous to fly.

As soon as I had finished talking to her the consultant and breast care nurse called Andrew and I through to the consulting rooms. We headed to the same room where I recently had the diagnosis feedback. "Can't we all sit in different places because it wasn't good news the last time we sat like this?" I asked. The consultant smiled then gave me a concerning look and answered, "It doesn't matter where we sit I have some bad news." Oh no, not again I thought. A heat began to rise up the back of my neck as he told us that not all the cancer had been taken in the first operation.

He was going to have to operate on me again and take more from the top and side of the cavity to see if we could get clearance. He continued to say that he had taken twenty seven lymph glands away and the cancer was only detected in two of them, which was good news. I tried to focus on the positive but asked if there was need to have taken them all away. The answer was yes, they had to all go for complete clearance. I had every faith in my consultant; I had heard many good things about his work and trusted he knew what he was doing for my benefit.

He continued to say that if we don't get clearance the next time then we should think about having the whole breast removed. My sister-in-law Maggie had recently gone through this experience and she was so encouraging at this time. Just observing how she had coped with this situation and come through it greatly helped. We found it hard to believe that both brothers had married women who ended up having breast cancer within a year of each other.

My poor husband! I looked at him as he tried to be strong for me again. We felt gutted, my poor parents and children. We had to go through it all again. It was like pressing re-play on a part of a film that you don't want to see again.

The Consulting Room

I sent a text to friends saying that I needed major prayers now! Once again friends and family were so supportive. I lay in bed that night praying for strength to get through this next round. I really felt that we were still in the surgery part of the journey and just hadn't ticked the box to get to the next thing on our list to overcome. I wasn't sure how long we would have to stay here but I was determined to get through it.

Storms and Blessings

6

My New Look

I lay on the bed the next morning just trying to take in what had been said to me. I had also been advised to prepare for my future treatments so this was the day I had an appointment to choose a wig. I dressed and went to pick up my mum. It was a strange experience because at this stage you can't imagine looking any different. I tried a couple on and just couldn't comprehend having no hair. The wigs didn't sit correctly because I still had my own hair. It didn't take long to choose one that was identical to my long brown hair and felt pleased that people wouldn't be able to tell. After this experience I just wanted to go home and take some headache tablets. I had talked about choosing a wig to a friend and laughed about going blonde and trying different styles, but when it actually happened I just wanted to choose one and get out of there.

Once I got home I lay on the bed; I was shattered, my body felt quite weak. I picked up my Bible and turned to Psalms, every word I read was an encouragement to praise God through various circumstances. It was not a natural feeling to praise God in these difficult situations but soon I began to just thank Him for what He was going to do and praised Him for keeping me strong and safe. The following day I felt so much better in my mind and spirit. It was a very hard lesson to learn but I strongly felt that God was teaching me to praise Him during the most difficult times in my life. I remembered hearing about a man who wrote a praise song after his family had been killed in a car crash. I felt that I was being taught the same lesson.

My daily reading said, *"If there is anything praiseworthy...meditate on these things"* (Philippians 4:8) Can you believe it? What I had felt yesterday about praising God through my low days was confirmed today. Wow! Jesus said, *"Your eye...provides light for your body. When your eye is good your whole body is filled with light. But when your eye is bad, your whole body is filled with darkness,"* (Matthew 6:22-23). My daily reading asked the question – What are you looking at? Each day you get to decide where you'll focus. You won't have to look far to find things to complain about. In the Bible it talks about God dividing the Red Sea, sending a sign to the Israelites in the wilderness and providing food so they'd never grow hungry. Initially *"...they sang his praise,"* but *"...soon forgot what He had done,"* (Psalm 106:12,13). We must try our best not to be like that. I reminded myself again *"...if there is anything praiseworthy...meditate on these things."* Surely I could find something to praise God for today.

My New Look

I thought about this and I had so many things to praise God for – my family, friends, that the condition I had was treatable even though it was classed as life threatening, that I was having strength at this time to cope with the situation, for the support I was getting, for my wonderful breast care nurse and surgeon. The list could go on. Praise God!

One of the songs I began to sing and listen to was *Shackles* by Mary, Mary. Some of the words in the song say, *"Take the shackles off my feet so I can dance. I just want to praise you, I just want to praise you."* I even began to dance and lift my hands in the privacy of my bedroom! I felt uplifted and a great release, I think I had learnt my lesson! My dad had mentioned the day before to keep raising my hands to praise God and you'll soon get your arm working again. It was definitely a good physiotherapy workout for that day!

Soon the time approached for my second operation. I felt very apprehensive and prayed I would get on with the people in my room. That ended up not being a problem at all. I began to look forward to my premed! But this time as soon as I had taken it the porter came to get me with a wheelchair. I hadn't even had time to lie down and enjoy the spaced out feeling. He left me sitting in the corridor on a wheelchair for a while as he arranged for a nurse to walk down to the theatre with us. I thought that if he left me for too long he may find me curled up on the floor asleep! Well, by the time I went to theatre the premed had started working. I climbed up on the operating trolley and as I lay down I noticed how comfortable and cosy the trolley was! I kept repeating it so much that the nurse and anaesthetist began laughing and said they had never had anyone saying that the operating table was the most comfortable trolley ever! The premed had definitely started working! Apparently, after the operation it had taken them longer to wake me up than normal, I did comment when I came around that I do love to sleep. The operation this time wasn't as major and I didn't have any drains.

A breast care nurse came to the ward to change my dressings. I felt quite alarmed when she told me that they had put a sticky pad all over my stitches and if she tried to pull it off she would pull out my stitches. This worried me greatly, my imagination worked overtime and I dreaded going for my next change of dressing. I imagined them having to re-stitch me. I suddenly remembered the verse *"Do not worry about tomorrow, for tomorrow will care for itself,"* Matthew 6:34. I prayed this prayer, "Lord if you can do one thing for me this week, take away the stickiness from my dressing, so it comes off easily."

Soon the day arrived when I was due to go to the breast care unit for the change of dressing. I took a high sugar drink, to up my sugars ready for my ordeal and a lolly to bite on! It wasn't unusual for me to feel faint in situations like this. I explained what had happened to my nurse Ann and she was wonderful, she encouraged me and said we would do it slowly and see what was going on. As she took off the first layer, I thought, here goes, the next layer she has to take off is the sticky pad. The nurse and my mum said there was nothing else to be removed! The sticky pad had come off with the dressing that had already been taken off! The pad had lost its stickiness, just like I had prayed! A weight was taken from

My New Look

my shoulders, thank you Lord.

Storms and Blessings

7

Healing Rain

Once again, we began to wait for the results. I had a feeling that all was not going to be alright this time again. The waiting is always an anxious time. Sitting in the waiting area for your appointment is the worst feeling but it's a great laxative! Soon it was our turn; we were taken into the same consulting room. Oh no, I thought – here we go again. The consultant looked at me and I just knew it wasn't good. "I'm afraid," he said, "I haven't got good news." He continued to tell me that we still didn't have clearance and he was starting to get anxious about the amount of time that was passing since I was diagnosed. He wanted me to go on to chemotherapy as soon as possible and then have blasts of radiotherapy in the areas that hadn't had clearance. Andrew and I struggled to understand this – we had our minds set that we would get total clearance and then move on. Suddenly, everything we thought would happen was changing. We asked many, many questions. The consultant was concerned that the cancer had gone to my lymph glands and it was very important to have chemo soon to kill any stray cells that might be in my body. We understood that and began to feel his eagerness to move on, but still concerned that we hadn't had clearance.

We were told that this decision was to be taken to the main meeting that week with the oncologist, radiologists etc where they discussed every patient. We had already talked ourselves into accepting these new decisions. We had been told that there was no time for a mastectomy, as you needed longer time to heal before starting chemotherapy.

We began to get quite anxious about the conclusions that were being made in this meeting. You just have to trust that these professionals make the correct decision for you. Soon we received the phone call from my nurse, after the meeting. We were to hear that the plans had changed again!

Apparently, all my personal data, percentages etc had been put into their computer and they had debated about me for a long time. It was eventually decided that there was time for me to have another incision to take more away, to try and get clearance again and regardless of this third operation result I would move on to chemotherapy. If the result still didn't have clearance, I was to have a mastectomy after chemo. Andrew and I felt much better with this decision because at the end of it all, regardless of how it would happen, I would have clearance. We were learning that not everyone follows the same journey in order to get clearance, for us there were no short cuts!

Healing Rain

Now I would have to pack my hospital bag again. I could do this with my eyes closed now! I just prayed – Lord, I need even more strength please. The nurses on the ward were so surprised to see me again. I decided to be brave this time and not have a premed!

I wasn't expecting it, but this operation was quite exhausting, I did feel as if all my energy had been taken from me. The anaesthetic really took any energy I had away. I felt very weak and emotional. I was surrounded by people in the room that had minor illnesses and I was the worst! They were all so shocked when I told them what I was in for. They would look at me with great pity and I felt as if I was the one to say I would be ok. When you are going through the same operations and treatment as people around you, you can get so inspired by others and that spurs you on. I realised how important that was on my journey through breast cancer, it is so important to have positive people surrounding you and people you can relate to.

Whilst on the ward I listened a lot to my i-pod. One of the songs that inspired me was *Healing Rain* by Michael W Smith, I really felt God close to me whenever I listened to it. I'm sure God has a sense of humour because every time I listened to the song a tremendous downfall of rain would happen outside, not just a shower but a downpour! This time there was thunder and lightening as well! I felt that God was showing me that when His healing rain falls it isn't going to be a little shower but a tremendous downpour where people would be saturated with His healing rain – dripping, saturated, soaked! This was very exciting and spurred me on to get through this stage.

Once more, after my operation it was waiting time again. Anxiety crept in but I felt as if I was being prepared for the results not to be clear again. On the day of the results, before going to see the consultant, I stopped Andrew as we were leaving the house and said not to be surprised if he says I have to have a mastectomy because I really felt we were heading in that direction. When we arrived my wonderful breast nurse had arranged for us to go into a different consulting room. I think we had spent too long in the other one! We looked at the consultant; he said that although we were in a different room, he still didn't have good news for me. This time I really wasn't surprised, apparently they had found numerous cancer cells in this part of the breast that had been taken away. Therefore, I was to start chemotherapy the following week, if my wound had healed sufficiently, and have a mastectomy after the chemo, as previously arranged.

Everyone I spoke to was "gutted for us", some people who had been praying for us even wondered what God was doing! But I stood by what I felt from the beginning – I had to go through the worst experience of breast cancer i.e. a mastectomy to be able to say at the end, "Look what God has brought me through, and He can do the same for you." If I could just inspire one person because of my journey, it would be worth it.

My nurse gave me a list of items that would help me as I went through chemotherapy. I will share them with you in the hope it may help someone who needs a few tips when preparing for what I experienced:

*   Thermometer – I found it was worth spending a bit more money on an ear monitor – it was the best and quickest because if my temperature went over 37.5 I had to phone the hospital.

*   Pineapple in own juice. I found this took away the certain metal taste that is on the roof of your mouth and cleansed my palette. I kept some in the fridge continually!

*   Ginger root – good for nausea feeling.

*   I had to stop using my electric toothbrush and use a soft toothbrush with sensitive toothpaste. A mouth wash I had from the doctor was fantastic for soreness and ulcers in the mouth. When I had ulcers I had to avoid citrus fruit as well.

*   My intake of water had to rise to two and a half – three litres a day.

*   I found I had to avoid strong cooking smells, for example cabbage, haddock and smells that linger. I found I had to stop using a certain washing powder and hand wash because the smell was too strong.

*   My immunity was going to drop so I had to avoid people with coughs and colds and use antibacterial gels on my hands and for the family.

*   My intake of fibre had to increase in my diet for a few days before my chemo sessions as they can make you constipated.

*   I had to start listening to my body and rest when I needed to.

*   Keep a diary about what helps on a daily basis. I took note of my temperature and tablets taken and things that disagreed with me!

*   I wasn't allowed to colour my hair or use hot straightening irons, even the hair dryer had to be cool and be gentle when brushing, to avoid pulling on hair.

*   I was encouraged to set little goals, like having a meal out, to focus on something positive. I found this was essential.

*   When you get a wig, remember to take it off when you open the oven door. I singed mine!

The lead up to chemotherapy is indescribable. For me, it was the complete unknown, how was I going to react, and you just cannot prepare yourself. One of the appointments I had to attend was to see the oncologist before I began my treatment. She went through all the known side effects and I had to sign a consent form with a whole list of them written on it. As I signed the paper, the consultant must have seen my face and said, "You don't have to have these entire side effects mind. I don't want you ticking all these boxes!" We laughed, as I looked at the page that was full of side effects!

I was very anxious the day before chemotherapy started, I couldn't relax at all. I felt quite nauseous all day. I couldn't believe it – I was having side effects before even starting the treatment! This was surely the wrong way around. But that night, I was inspired by a friend who put a card through the door with these verses written on it:

He who dwells in the shelter of the Most High will rest in the shadow of the Almighty. I will say of the Lord, "He is my refuge and my fortress, my God, in whom I trust." Surely he will save you from the fowler's snare and from the deadly pestilence. He will cover you with his feathers, and under his wings you will find refuge; his faithfulness will be your shield. You will not fear the terror of the night, nor the arrow that flies by day, nor the pestilence that stalks in the darkness, nor the plague that destroys at midday.......He will command his angels concerning you to guard you in all your ways; they will lift you up in their hands, so that you will not strike your foot against a stone.

Psalm 91

If you know someone going through a similar experience, words of encouragement are so important. You can be God's mouthpiece with the right words at the right time.

8

Chemo Blast

The day arrived. I woke up with a feeling of relief, at last we were going to start treatment. My husband showed great concern for me; he kept hugging me and asking if I was ok. I replied, "I am, but are you?" It's so hard for loved ones looking on, including children and parents. I personally had to have the strength to deal with it; I was the one having the chemicals pumped into my body. I had to be focused and positive and not look at the "what ifs." I was occupied! You almost become blinkered. But for loved ones, they can't do anything to help, apart from just be there and stay positive with you.

It is a very emotional time for them and I thank the Lord that I'm in a great supportive family. My brother even travelled back from Australia before I started chemo. It was great to see him and it was good for him to see that I wasn't bedridden. When something like this happens you realise how far away

Australia is, but when he returned, we made sure we kept him informed of every part of my journey.

My dad was a brilliant chauffeur that day and every day of my chemo. I was driven in style to the hospital. My mum was my chemo partner, I'd heard of a birthing partner but this was something else! She had such strength, it was amazing to see. I thank God for my wonderful parents. As we arrived at the doors, I took a deep breath and said, "Let's go for it!" As we entered the reception area, the first person we saw was a friend's sister, who put us at ease immediately. All the staff there were lovely and caring. The ladies who were in the waiting area were encouraging and we all had a story to tell. I immediately noticed that their wigs were impressive. I couldn't imagine wearing one continually at this stage but I knew the time would come.

The chemo I was due to have was TAC, (taxotere, adriamycin and cyclophosphamide) my nurse had warned me that they would blast me. It was going to be a steel top to toe job! The nurse sat with me and explained the side effects I could have. They started pumping one part of the chemo into my vein at a time. I was fine until they started giving me taxotere of the chemo. I felt an intense heat rising up my face. The nurse had her back to me at this moment and mum had gone to the toilet. When I called out to her to see if what I was experiencing was normal she looked at me and immediately turned off the drip. She went to get the doctor to come and see me. My stomach turned, I prayed, "Please Lord, let me be able to have the chemo." I started to get concerned. My poor mum saw the doctor coming to see someone, not realising it was me. She walked in to see the doctor and nurse standing over me. She commented that she only went out for two minutes and I decided to play up! The other lady having chemo in the same room as me said my face was the colour of a beetroot!

They decided to give me a little break and pump it into me at a slower rate. Thank the Lord, this worked and my body was able to cope with it that way. As I sat there, an older man in the opposite room, also having treatment kept waving at me. I smiled and waved back. We continued to have the treatment and when he had finished he came into my room and was a great encouragement. He said he had watched me and I had been an inspiration to him. He thought I had come with someone else, to be a support, then realised it was me having the chemo! He bent down and asked what my secret was to being so positive and not looking miserable! I replied that I had a great supportive family and my faith helped me a great deal. He agreed and said he also went to a church and found that his faith was a great support.

Everyone in the chemo unit was so encouraging, even the Red Cross ladies who provide drinks and sandwiches had a smile. As soon as I went home I took another anti-sickness tablet. I stayed home, not knowing what was going to happen to me. As the afternoon went by I felt nausea but not terribly, but by 7pm the nausea took over. The thought of any food turned me and just walking into the kitchen made me heave. By 8.40pm I had started to vomit, but after that I began to feel better. I spent most of the night going back and forth to the toilet – not to vomit but just through the extra amount of fluid intake. I began to have very intense flushes. By the morning my temperature had begun to rise but not to the point of having to phone the hospital. I was truly hot stuff! My cheeks were beetroot red; it was the side effect of something. But which tablet or part of chemo, I wasn't sure. Soon my temperature had begun to go down with the help of my trusted electric fan!

My parents called around to see me, bringing Arrow Root biscuits which is meant to be good for nausea (helps with morning sickness in pregnancy as well!) That day I started my steroids, I was expecting to have heaps of energy after taking them. At this point I just didn't want to go out anywhere because I wasn't sure of what was going to happen to me. You tend to sit and wait for the side effects to happen. The days are just so unpredictable at this early stage. I just didn't want to start vomiting in shops! Sadly the reams of energy I thought I would have with the steroids never came.

As the day passed, it really hit me the reality of having chemo. After this first session, just not knowing how my body would react was concerning. My energy levels were quite low and I would watch the clock and feel relieved when ten minutes then half an hour, then an hour had gone by without vomiting. Then you hold your breath while you face the next hour to see what that brings. I continually felt nausea, it intensified again and a strange metallic taste was in my mouth, it even felt strange on my lips. It's a disgusting taste! I supped mints, lollies, fresh pineapple, anything to have a different taste in my mouth. I began to think that I was going to go up the scales and put on weight very quickly if this carried on. It was then I decided I would be concerned about my weight gain after this was all over. I had to get through this treatment in any way I could and if that was going to be eating something continually then so be it!

I found I had to go to bed so early, my temperature would start rising and I would feel a heat rising to boiling point in my body. I felt as if I was being cooked from the inside out! The fan was continually on; my husband had to put up with frosty toes! I found the mornings were particularly difficult, as I had to try and focus on getting dressed and pull myself together after such restless nights. The loss of energy and every time you move anywhere a wave of nausea hits you, isn't pleasant. Lord, what is going on?! I felt as if I was in a chemo circle and I couldn't get out. I couldn't get rid of this intense feeling.

Amazingly, four days after having my first chemo I was able to make a Sunday roast for the family and clean downstairs. I felt so pleased I had been able to do something normal. I felt re-energised until the next morning! What had I done? My temperature rose and I had minus zero energy. I could hardly talk to my husband. I couldn't even concentrate on putting a sentence together. I lay on the settee all day and didn't move. My parents phoned to see how I was and I could hardly speak. It was then I realised and began to accept that I couldn't do everything on one day again. I had to learn to pace myself, even when I felt as if I had a bit more energy. My breast care nurse phoned me to see how I was and she confirmed what I was feeling. I had done too much and the chemo knocked my energy levels low again very quickly.

Storms and Blessings

This was a lesson that I had to learn throughout all my treatment. My life at this stage had surely changed already.

9

My Angel

The week after my first chemo my temperature rose to 38, I was suffering with a sore throat and earache. If your temperature rises to this you are told to contact the hospital. I decided to phone the chemo day unit first to get advice. There was no hesitation on the telephone; they wanted to admit me straight away. I had to pack an overnight bag and they said a bed would be waiting for me on the ward. My stomach turned – what were the people going to be like on the cancer ward? Was it going to upset me?

As I entered the ward, my details and blood tests were taken very quickly. Soon I found out that I had become neutropenic, my neutrophils had dropped down to zero. I had absolutely no immune system, they told me I could be in hospital for up to seven days, depending on my blood, which would be checked daily. I was immediately put on an intravenous drip of antibiotics. The first couple of days I felt extremely drained, I developed spots on my body and face, which is always a sign that I am run down. My mum helped to shower me as I wasn't allowed to get my intravenous line wet. As she washed my hair, the first signs of hair loss could be seen. You start to begin to take notice of hair left on your brush and in the shower plug hole.

In a couple of days I began to feel more uplifted physically and I had good news that my count had risen to 0.7. Then suddenly I felt very faint and extra fluids had to be pumped into me immediately. I started to feel very unwell but little did I know that God had planned a wonderful experience to happen that very night.

I was getting ready for bed, I went to close the curtains around my area and I suddenly felt God's presence in my area. I looked at my chair, which was next to the bed and felt such peace – there was an angel sitting right next to my bed! I couldn't see it physically but I could have drawn an outline of where it was. It was huge and was as high as the bedside curtains. In my spirit I just felt God saying, "I am here with you, I will be with you all night." I lay in bed and felt the presence of God surrounding me in a very intense way. It was wonderful. I soaked it all up! I listened once again to *Healing Rain* by Michael W Smith. God's presence went up and down my body like waves. I felt as if tomorrow I was going to feel so much better.

I slept like a baby all night. The nurse who had been on night time duty came in to do the usual morning checks on me. I told her how well I had slept. She said, "We had such an unusually peaceful night last night, no one called or buzzed and everyone I have checked this morning has said they have had a great night's sleep." I laughed and said it was because the angels were here last night. She agreed with me!

My daily blood test was taken and my neutrophils had risen from 0.7 to 2.5 overnight. I was immediately put on oral antibiotics instead of the intravenous drip and told I could be home the next day! I knew I had received a healing touch and the proof was in my blood tests. I felt one hundred per cent better; my nurse phoned me and said it can take at least a week for neutrophils to reach a normal mark, sometimes longer.

I phoned my parents and Andrew to share my great news, at the same time I was speaking to my husband, the hospital chaplain poked his head in at the door to say goodnight, at which point I shouted back, "God bless, darling!" "Oh, no," I said to Andrew, "I've just called the hospital chaplain darling!" We laughed. The funny thing was that the chaplain came back the next morning to say "Good morning" to me! I was more reserved in my response!

When I left the hospital on the next day, my levels had gone up to 5.2 – higher than before I started chemo! I was able to go out and do things after this hospital visit. The family saw such a difference in me. Praise the Lord!

Soon my scalp started to hurt and one morning I was washing my hair over the bath and slowly I could see the bath filling with my hair. This was quite traumatic for my girls to see. My youngest girl began to cry, "Oh, mum, I don't want your hair to go." I promised them that I would be the same person and cover my head if it upset them too much. She made me "pinkie promise" not to go out with a bald head! That promise, I would always keep for the girls' sake. The three of us hugged each other and cried in the bathroom together. Once again, I found myself explaining that this had to happen to make me better.

Chloe suggested reading the story we first had on my initial diagnosis *Mummy's Lump* to her sister, to help her understand. She was acting in such a mature manner, I was so proud of them both. Shona commented that the picture in the story of the mum with a bald head was scary. I hugged her and said I wouldn't be scary and focused her attention on my hair growing back. Chloe confessed that she would be embarrassed if I went out with a bald head like that. I was so fortunate that my girls were able to express their innermost worries, so we could deal with them straight away.

Helen came to the house bearing gifts of scarves and hats. She had gone on the internet and ordered from a specific site for hair loss. I was so touched by her generosity and care. I found it an emotional experience when I tried them on but so relieved I had something to cover my head apart from a wig. My girls and I tried them on and had a giggle together the next day. They began to relax when they saw how my head could be covered. I promised again that I wouldn't go out without covering my head. I even had night caps, so in the mornings the girls didn't have to worry and my husband didn't have to stare at my bald head!

It got to the point of every morning waking up to find a layer of hair on my pillow. When I would dress I would find strands of hair on my clothes. It was at this time my hair really began to fall out. I had long hair at this stage and decided I needed a drastic short cut. My girls didn't like my new hair style, but it was good preparation before my total hair loss for them and me. I cried myself to sleep one night – just with all the physical changes that were happening and with what everyone was dealing with. Once again, my Bible brought great comfort, I read how God will bring you through because He's *"The God of all comfort,"* 2 Corinthians 1:3. I was reminded that God can bring you through the situations in which you think you won't survive, He can bring peace in the midst of trauma. He says, *"I will lead them in paths they have not known. I will make darkness light before them, and crooked places straight. These things I will do for them, and not forsake them,"* Isaiah 42:16. I was reminded that He was with me, even in my lowest times. I read Psalm 30:5 that *"Weeping may endure for the night, but joy comes in the morning."* I felt that God was with me every step of the way and it was amazing how directly He spoke to me at the times I needed comfort, security and protection.

As I saw my hair falling out, I felt as if I was being stripped away of all my familiar facial features. What others would think of as a woman's outward beauty – hair, eyebrows, eyelashes etc. As I stood over my bedroom bin putting in more hair, it hit me that inward beauty really is far more important. Although my outward appearance was changing drastically, I was still the same person; my personality wasn't going to change. I was still loved and I still loved the same family and friends, no matter what.

Storms and Blessings

10

Goodbye Hair

My hair began to go extremely patchy; I developed a bald patch at the top of my head. This really upset my husband as it made me look ill. He decided he would go and get our friend's hair shaver to shave it off! We discussed it and both agreed now was the time to do it as I was having pain in my scalp and felt as if my hair was like bristles on my head. It really hurt! We had a laugh while he was doing it. I was so jumpy; I thought he may shave the top of my ear off! He was very brave to do the deed, but we both felt a great relief after he had done it. It was done, my hair had gone. He said I looked so much better than having patches. Then I looked in the mirror! What a shock! I was ok till I walked away, then I burst into tears. It just confirmed the reality of everything I was going through. The tears didn't last long, my husband hugged me straight away, he kept saying I had such a beautiful face and it didn't matter. He even said I had a nice shaped head! At which point I burst out laughing. At this early stage of hair loss I found wearing head scarves around the house really helped. I could cope with the baldness much better.

We had to go and see the oncologist that afternoon, so I went upstairs to put on my wig and hat for the first adventure outdoors. I took off the scarf I was wearing and looked in the mirror. I let out a shocked squeal; I had forgotten how drastic the change was! But then I laughed at my reaction and put on my wig. If that was my reaction – what would others think?!

We had good news at the hospital – my neutrophils had gone up to 6.0. Such a massive rise compared to before my first chemo. Thank God for my neutrophil angel and a healing touch. The oncologist decided that I would go on to antibiotics five days after my chemo to try and keep my neutrophils from falling again, as he really wanted to keep the chemo levels the same. If I dropped again, he would have to change the levels of chemo I was having, but he reassured me it wouldn't change the final result. We felt fine about this decision.

My girlies came home and wanted to see my hair; Andrew had prepared them and told them he had shaved it off. I slowly revealed my bald head but I still had some bristles. Chloe wanted to touch it first, and then Shona said, "Yuk, it feels like daddy's chin!" I was so proud of them. They didn't like it but they also felt relieved that we had got to the end of this losing hair episode and now we had to get on with the process. Once again they needed reassurance that I wouldn't go out in public with a bald head.

Goodbye Hair

My second chemo session was fast approaching and I had a good week before it was due. I was feeling positive and refreshed. I braved myself to wear my wig without a hat to chemo. I was very encouraged when the nurse asked me if I wanted the cold cap on my head to save my hair! I laughed and said, "Too late, I've already lost it all." It can't have looked that bad after all. I went through this chemo session without any hitches. But when I got home I was hit with a feeling of fatigue that was indescribable. It lasted for nearly a week. I could walk downstairs, after wondering for an hour how I was going to get out of bed in the morning. I lay on the settee; it was an effort to even speak on the phone to my parents daily. I could just say I was ok but had zero energy. I couldn't concentrate for long enough to even have a conversation. The feeling was awful, heaviness was on my legs and I wondered how I would move, even to the toilet.

The feeling started to lift from me six days later and I heard Andrew commenting to a friend on the phone that I was speaking again! I was so excited to be on my feet, I cooked tea for everyone and enjoyed doing it. Then the high temperature hit me again. I lay on the bed knowing what was coming. Chloe got concerned when she saw it had risen. We talked and I calmed her down, telling her there was nothing to worry about. It just meant I had to go into hospital for a few days. The following morning my temperature hadn't gone down. I knew I had to make the phone call to the hospital. A bed was made available for them to do tests on me again. I was on an intravenous drip for fluids and antibiotics immediately. My blood test results came back to say my white cells and neutrophils had dropped again. This time I was 0.1, it hadn't quite gone down to zero this time. I thought here we go again. I prayed for God to touch me once more.

Although I was in hospital, I did experience some funny moments. As I was settling down in my bed a nurse came into the room huffing and puffing. I asked her what the matter was. She said she had just looked in the mirror and noticed the state of her hair. I burst out laughing and said, "don't complain, at least you have some!" As I got ready to go to sleep, I lay there smiling, remembering a conversation I had the night before, with my husband about my night cap. We had a good laugh at the caps; I looked like an old man or woman in a pink lacy cap. I could never put it on right, so I always looked funny. I said to him that he must find every girl with hair attractive at the minute! He replied, "You know what; I've actually told some people I think you look sexy with no hair, you are beautiful!" What a husband! As usual my eyes filled with tears and I replied, "No way!" We laughed as he smoothed my head. We agreed that if we can get through this, we can get through anything.

My dad phoned me in hospital to say that while he had been praying the Holy Spirit had come. He called to tell me to lie down and see what God would do. I did, and was surrounded by His peace and reassurance. I was praying and listening to my music, when suddenly one nurse walked into my room shouting, "Wake up, you lazy b******, I've come to wash your private bits!"

Sorry Lord, I thought and laughed. I also replied that she wasn't going to touch my private bits and we laughed. Talk about a change in atmosphere! She put the curtains around the older lady next to me and while the lady was bending over to be washed, the nurse said in a very loud voice, "Now I know where I can park my bike!" We all burst out laughing in the room, even the older lady! What a nurse!

The lady next to me was ninety one years old, she was lovely and I ended up helping her a few times. I would ask her every morning how she was feeling. This one particular morning, she woke up quite concerned. She said she wasn't sure if she had dreamt it but last night she told me she opened her eyes and saw a man in black nodding to her at the end of the bed. She thought it was Batman! I laughed and informed her it had been the hospital chaplain! We laughed so much. They say laughter is the best medicine.

Storms and Blessings

11

Take A Break

I was advised by a friend who had been through chemo that when you are feeling strong it is good to go away for a couple of days, just to get away from everything and have a break. We were blessed that a friend from work offered us his local timeshare villa and other friends from church offered us their log cabin, we were so grateful. It was just what we needed and not too far away. It was lovely to spend time away from the chemo circle I was in. Yet, it highlighted to me how much I wasn't up to my full potential. I could only go out for a short time, sometimes just a car journey would wear me out and I would then sit in the car whilst Andrew took the girls exploring. I needed to come back to our log cabin for a rest and sleep so I had the energy to go out for tea. It is a great learning curve, to try and listen to your own body and only do what you know you can, even if it is very limited. I physically couldn't push myself to do any more, otherwise I would feel really ill but I enjoyed the break, and the times I could go out were a boost for me. It was great to see the smiles on my girls' faces when they came back from adventures with Andrew.

One beautiful sunny afternoon, Andrew took the girls to the pool that was in the complex. I said I would meet them later, as I couldn't stay for the whole session. I walked down slowly in my jeans, T-shirt and sun hat, to shield my bald head. When I got there, everyone else had on their bathers. Tears began to run down my face as I sat in the shade. Everyone looked normal, except me. I was having a weak moment! Andrew hugged me when we got back to the log cabin and said, "How do you know everyone there was normal?" Once again he made me laugh and reminded me that this was for a season and we would get through it.

In my good week before the next chemo, I had a boost, as I was able to go to a friend's wedding. They were so kind and said if I woke up and felt I couldn't make it, they'd understand. This was my worry, because on chemo I learnt you can't make future plans because you don't know how you are going to feel on a daily basis. You don't want to let people down but I soon realised that my friends understood. I knew I couldn't make it to the church service and the reception, so Andrew came to get me for the reception. Once again this was a time of listening to my own body and admitting the limits of it. Otherwise I would have spent the following week in bed, if I'd overdone it. It was great to see friends who were so encouraging, although some wonderful comments brought tears to my eyes; friends were so good to me. My friend, who had also experienced the reality of chemo, compared wigs with me in the ladies; it's comical what becomes normal so quickly. As I was leaving after the reception, I had to struggle to hold onto my emotions when the father of the bride hugged me and said, "You don't know how much you have made our day with your effort to be here today. I really mean that." Well, I nearly burst into tears, I was so touched.

I was very tired for a few days after that but it was certainly worth it. Shona actually prayed one night, "Lord, please give mummy more energy. She used to be able to run around the yard twice. I don't know if she can even run around half of it at the minute!"

It's a strange feeling getting to half way of the chemo treatments. I felt relieved, yet you know you've got to do the same thing over again. It had been decided that my chemo was to be reduced. I was very nauseous this time; I was warned that there would be a build up in my body. I experienced the fatigue which lasted for five days. My girls got upset when they saw I couldn't get out of bed. I didn't have the energy to get dressed. I didn't even have the energy to put on a front while the girls were with me and pretend I was feeling stronger. That feeling knocked me down for a few days. I cried – I felt as if I couldn't fulfil the role of a wife or mother. Poor Andrew had to do everything. I cried and said I was sorry to put him through this. As ever he said he didn't mind and that it would be all over soon. But it felt like ages to me!

On the days I couldn't get out of bed to make my own breakfast, my girls would make it for me and serve me in bed. They would walk into the bedroom with big smiles on their faces and stay to make sure I ate every bit of my cereal. They were fantastic! This also helped with my nausea, if I ate before getting up, it wasn't as intense. But soon my strong days came again. The girls could see I was just having my bad days and then I began to feel stronger again, they were so pleased that I didn't have to go to hospital this time. Chloe was on a high and kept hugging me; whenever I took my temperature she would hold her breath in anticipation! I tried not to take it in front of the girls – just in case, but Shona liked to pretend that she was a nurse and took all our temperatures! I was so proud of how the girls had coped so far with everything that had happened. I prayed they would be stronger girls because of this experience and realise they can cope in different situations, even at their young ages.

I seemed to feel stronger for longer before my next chemo blast, this time. But I began to feel sick even before having my next chemo treatment! I reacted to the steroids I took the day before my treatment. My cheeks and chin were so flushed. I looked like a bald red raspberry! They didn't give me extra steroids on the day of my treatment as they could see the effect on my face.

Once again I felt nausea for the first couple of days and by Monday I was totally wiped out with fatigue. My skin and bones began to feel so sensitive and my legs felt like lead. I'd even began hallucinating this time whilst asleep. I thought my mum was in the room and I actually woke up speaking to her, then realised she wasn't there! I didn't like those experiences; my dreams became vivid and so real. I had hot sweats in the night then I would get really cold, I had continual restless nights.

One night Shona came into our room at 3am saying she had a bad dream. I hugged and kissed her and went to lie in her bed to settle her again. It suddenly hit me that no matter how low, with or without hair, thin or fat, I was still needed by my children. They had an undying love for me which was unconditional. It didn't matter what I looked like to them, they still needed me. Importance of looks and appearance is immaterial when real love is there.

I was beginning to experience another lesson in life, that when we are stripped away of looks, our outward appearance, what other people think of as normal, we are only left with what God sees – the true inward parts. We live in such an appearance driven society that focuses on the outward instead of our spiritual condition. I learnt to surround myself with true, honest friends and family, who lift you up when you feel low. I pray that I will be more a heart orientated person than appearance driven. Yes, it's good to look after yourself but I feel as if going to the supermarket without any make up on isn't so bad after all! I may even try it now!

Storms and Blessings

12

A Bridge to Blessings

Once again, I felt sick before having the next chemo. The thought of it just turned my stomach but the nurses in the chemo unit are so encouraging and sensitive, they put me at ease immediately. Even the Red Cross ladies once again had smiles on their faces when they supplied us with crisps and sandwiches (well, my mum – I couldn't face them!) They were all such a blessing.

The same routine happened again, nausea for the first couple of days then the fatigue set in. This time I felt as if it took longer to get over, in actual fact I didn't have a good week before my next chemo. My bones were so stiff, aching and sore, my hands were so stiff that I couldn't grip things properly. I felt as if I was in my nineties when I tried to get up from a chair! I couldn't wear any type of heels because my knees were so weak – they are usually a necessity when you are shorter. But not any more!

In my fatigued week, I was lying on the settee with no energy and turned on the God Channel and such an encouraging program was on for half an hour. It was amazing that throughout my treatments and operations that just when I needed a boost someone would say something, send a text or I would watch a program or read something and it would be just what I needed.

The man I watched spoke about God changing the barriers in our life into bridges to His blessings. Barriers can include health problems – He can change this into a situation that makes us trust Him more. God blesses you so you can then be a blessing. He said that whatever problem you are facing, it comes back to the cross of Jesus Christ. He gave His life so we could have a bridge to our blessings.

At the time, this was real confirmation about how I was feeling. I had to go through this and come out so much stronger when it was all over – spiritually and physically. I held on to this, even through the lowest points of my journey. There is a song we sing in church that says, "You are my strength when I am weak" and I can honestly say that I've experienced that first hand! The little spark I usually felt in my last week before the next chemo just wasn't there in my body this time. I felt weak but not bedridden. Chloe even asked when my good week was this time. I said we are in it and she looked shocked!

I read in Romans 8:18, *"I consider that our present sufferings are not worth comparing with the glory that will be revealed in us."* This really spurred me on, especially after having my blood test taken before my next chemo. The hospital phoned me to say my neutrophils were low and they weren't going to give me my next chemo until they had risen. This was going to be my last chemo and I really wanted to get it over with. I was told that I had to go to hospital an hour earlier than my planned chemo session to have more blood taken to see if they had risen at all. I sent texts to a few friends and asked family to pray. I was so disappointed initially but on the other hand the following week was going to be half term and it would make sure I had some good days with the girls, when I would be usually nauseous and fatigued. They said I may have to wait a week for the next session if my count was still low.

I went early to the chemo unit and had my blood tests; we had really prayed that my levels would rise to get it all over with. We waited patiently, and then my results came back. The nurse was so surprised, she commented, "Wow, your levels rise quickly, which is unusual!" Mum and I asked what she meant. She replied, "Your levels were 1.3 and they are 7.0 now!" I only had to rise to 1.5 for my chemo! She commented that she had never heard of a rise so quickly and high before. Mum and I looked at each other and gave each other a knowing smile. I replied, "It's an answer to prayer." God had once again done a miracle for me and proved the power of prayer really is amazing.

I had my sixth chemo as planned. At last I had finished! It was a peculiar feeling, saying goodbye to the nurses who had been such a support. Now I prayed that I would never see them again – only in the supermarket! But I have to say that the chemo nurses are very special people to work in that department.

Although my chemo had finished and friends began to text and phone to say congratulations – I still had to go through the side effects again. Once again the nausea, fatigue and terrible heart burn came. I felt quite dizzy at times, but some would say that is quite normal for me! I wished every hour away. The first week dragged by because I just wanted to feel normal again quickly. At times like this, one of my goals was looking forward to meeting my friends I had met in the hospital ward on my first operation. We would meet every three weeks on our "good week" for a coffee. We spurred each other on throughout our treatments and operations. They had become such good friends. We shared our stories of aches and pains, we encouraged each other, we laughed, we cried. We were there for each other throughout our whole experience; we all had a story to tell. My aim was to be better for this get together and enjoy my hot chocolate!

I also had more time to share with my parents and family. Mum and I were able to go out for an hour when I felt well enough. We can honestly look back and say it has been a time of laughter with my parents as well as a time of concern. My husband and I even became regulars at our local carvery! Before this experience, going out with him by ourselves was a novelty. I was even able to go to friends' houses for coffee in the day time! As a full time teacher this was a treat, even just picking up my children on a good day was an achievement. Friends from work and church came for a coffee. These were all little goals that helped me on my good days to feel normal throughout my treatment. I was truly enjoying spending time with the people who were most important in my life. I thank God for them all.

It was during my third week after the last chemo that I thought I saw my hair growing back again. My husband laughed and said he had more hair on his chin after he had shaved! But I was right; Chloe commented that when she kissed my head she could now feel hair. It was a little encouragement, my dad and mum even said they could see some growth. I knew people were entertaining me, but it was working!

My girls weren't well at the beginning of their half term holidays. Shona had a temperature of 39 C and was vomiting, whilst Chloe had tonsillitis. Oh Lord, I prayed, you need to protect me, considering I'm meant to be avoiding germs and viruses! I had a bottle of antibacterial spray on me continually! The children moved and I would spray! One day, my mum came sick visiting and thought it was unusual when she arrived that there was a smell of apples outside the house. She thought I couldn't be cooking an apple pie – it was my bad week! When she came in, she realised I had been spraying and the smell was even outside! It promised to kill 99.9% of viruses and I was turning into the antibacterial queen! It was amazing because I didn't catch one germ. Everyone around me, including my parents and husband all came down with viruses and God shielded me from them. My friend even commented that everyone she knew had a virus and I was the only one she knew who hadn't had anything!

Storms and Blessings

Slowly I recovered from my sixth chemo effects but it can be in your system for quite a while. I went to visit the oncologist who prescribed Tamoxifen, which regulates oestrogen being produced in my body. I have to take it for the next five years. I also visited my breast care nurse and consultant who would be giving me a mastectomy; we set a date for my operation. It was going to be three weeks after my last chemo. It was great to see them again as it confirmed to me that my chemo journey was over – a great relief.

13

The Big Op

Whilst on my visit to the breast care nurse she showed me the breast prosthesis I would wear after my surgery, then the different ones you can wear at different stages of healing. One even had a sticky back. Andrew asked if I would wear it at night. She said I could but there was a possibility he could wake up with it on him! What a giggle! But on the other side of this experience, it can be a very emotional time. She prepared me for the emotions I could feel after the operation. She said that some ladies experience a grieving process at losing a part of their body, which you can feel for many years. I joked and said my breasts have never played a big role in my life! But as she said, it doesn't matter if you are big or small; it is a part of you. She was lovely and caring and helped to bring out emotions I was ignoring.

This was a very sensitive time; I found it very difficult to prepare myself for a mastectomy. People would ask how I was feeling and I found it hard to put my emotions into words. On one hand, you feel that you should be thinking about it to prepare yourself and on the other, you don't want to bring yourself down. How was I really going to feel? I didn't really know, all I knew was it had to be done and this way I would be clear from the cancer that was there.

It's a strange sequence of events before the operation. You become more aware of your last shower, your last bath, the last time you get undressed for bed seeing your breast. I even found myself saying goodbye to it in the hospital the night before the operation. I found this to be so emotional. You want to make sure you've accepted what is going to happen to you. I trusted I was in the Lord's hands and I would be ok.

When I arrived at the hospital, to my surprise, I was put in a single room. I could antibacterial wipe till my heart was content! My parents could smell it when they came to visit! I had the usual checks and visits from medical staff. I made sure I ordered the premed for this operation. The main word that was on my heart for this time in hospital was "trust." I had to trust in the surgeons and trust in the Lord.

The day of the operation arrived and thankfully I was first on the list, with not much time to think about it. Before I knew it, I was in my backless gown and thigh high support stockings! What a look! Being in a single room, I couldn't embarrass myself during my premed or after the operation!

I was wheeled down to theatre praying for God just to help me get through it. I was still feeling weak after my chemo. The staff I had were wonderful, putting me at ease and before I knew it, I was coming around again.

The Big Op

I just remember feeling so cold, I was chattering and physically shuddering. They kept putting more blankets on me, which didn't seem to help. Soon I was back in my room where I was covered with more blankets. It was then the shudders stopped and peace took over. Soon my parents and Andrew arrived. As the days went on, I just didn't feel well at all. I was feeling nausea and if I sat in the chair beside my bed for the nurses to change my bed, I would have to sleep for a couple of hours. I put it down to the major operation and the extra anaesthetic I had.

But one night, it came to a head when my dad was visiting me. We chatted for half an hour, and then I felt this heaviness of sleep come over me. He read the paper, whilst I dozed for quarter of an hour. Suddenly I knew I wanted to be sick. I was! We buzzed for the nurses who came immediately and injected me with anti-sickness serum. They changed the bed and I started to feel faint like never before. It was a more intense, unwell feeling. I lay down and felt absolutely awful, then the lights in the room hurt my eyes. I had to keep them closed. Words just can't describe how I felt. My heart rate went up to 145 and my blood pressure dipped. Two doctors were called and bloods were taken. I was concerned in case I was bleeding internally. They mentioned that I may need a blood transfusion, if my count was low. I was trying to relax for my heart rate to go down, but every time I heard them say "Her heart rate is still very high", I felt as if I got worse!

My dad was fantastic, such a calming influence, although I knew by his face he was extremely concerned. I knew he was praying by my side. Everyone around us was so serious; I couldn't talk or open my eyes. I continued to feel dreadful. After two hours of close monitoring, the drips started to work and thankfully I didn't need a transfusion. We had a nasty fright at how ill I had become so quickly. My dad had phoned Andrew to say I had taken a dip and if he was needed my mum would go down to be with the children. Thank the Lord we didn't have to put that plan into action and the nurses said it was ok for dad to go home.

As the night went on I slowly began to feel more with the world again. I had three huge fluid bags pumped into me. They said I was dehydrated as well. By morning I was able to get out of bed slowly! After having to use the commode in the night with the help of a nurse, I was glad to be able to walk to the toilet unaided. My energy levels were very low but I was so glad to be able to stand again. The nurses were fantastic with me.

My breast care nurse was shocked when she saw my notes. There was no way now that I was going home soon. I didn't know how I would have walked out of the hospital anyway. Each day I began to improve and I saw more breast care patients coming in for operations then going home. One lady next door to me was in for reconstruction surgery. After her operation she was very proud to show off her new mountain! She commented that her new breast was called Pamela Anderson while the other was Nora Batty!

After a few days my breast care nurse said I was able to have my drains removed, this was such a relief, I was heading in the right direction now. We had named my two drains Ant and Dec! I ended up staying in hospital for eight days. At last

The Big Op

I had the energy and strength to walk out of hospital. My parents came to collect me and as I walked down the corridor I noticed how fast everyone was walking. Each person seemed to be rushing everywhere. Now I realise, it was because of how slow I was! But when you have been in a single room for eight days, the outside world seems very busy.

I started recovering at home. My girls and husband were so glad to have me home again. It was great to start feeling normal once more. It took a couple of weeks before I started to feel stronger in myself. I found that my stay in hospital had taken my confidence away to go out anywhere. I felt as if I had really achieved a goal on my first time out. After falling ill so quickly in the hospital I was scared it would happen again – but it didn't.

I had regular visits to my breast care nurse, who had to drain my bruising. My haemoglobins had dropped and I had become anaemic and was told this had caused my severe bruising around my wound. I had also developed, whilst in hospital, a very nasty bruise on my hip area on the same side as my operation. Apparently, it can be common in older people, where you can have pooling of blood from the operation. Well, I was feeling quite old! Whenever the nurse drained my wound I would never look. Andrew would, he was braver than me! I wanted to see it by myself first.

Storms and Blessings

14

Minus One

Soon the time came for me to take the dressing off and look at my... I didn't know what to call it anymore. I decided it was still my chest area, so that's what it still had to be called. My breast care nurse was wonderful, when in my morning visit I lay on the treatment bed. I didn't look but she took off the bandage and dressings and held my hand so I could feel the area. She asked me if I wanted to look – I didn't, not yet. I wanted to be at home as I didn't know how I would react. My husband had seen the area right from the initial dressing change to the draining of the area and watched everything. He was so supportive and brave! I will always be grateful to him for this at such an emotional time.

Straight from the hospital I went to meet my "bosom buddies" for our regular three week coffee and hot chocolate meeting. It was so encouraging to see them all again. We changed the name of our group throughout our experience. At one point we were "the wigs" and towards the end of our experience we were the "Costa girls." Two had lumpectomies and one had a mastectomy before chemotherapy and radiotherapy. We were able to chat and share anxieties and feelings, it was so encouraging. As the day went on I longed to lie in the bath again without the dressings on. I knew this could happen now. I had to be brave and take the dressing off. My nurse had advised me that when I did it for the first time to cover the other breast and not look in the mirror, but look down initially. I followed her every word. My eldest daughter had started to nag that she wanted to see it.

I went to the quietness of my bedroom and did it when everyone was occupied. I slowly took off the dressing and there I stood looking at myself, I didn't cry but felt a relief that now I had seen it and didn't have to dread the moment anymore. This was me now; I was still the same person but just looked different in one area of my body. As I looked I thought this had to happen for me to survive. I had no choice, so I must carry on. Obviously, it is an emotional experience; no one could possibly go through this and feel no emotions.

I showed my daughter who wanted to see it. We had all gone through this experience as a close family. I couldn't hide anything from them. This was how I looked now and we all had to slowly get used to it together, step by step.

As the days passed I slowly grew stronger, I wasn't my new self yet. I had a long way to go. Each day was a learning time, to discover how much or little I could do. I began to just go up to my parents' house for a little while then slowly I began to go further. Just an hour at the shops wore me out. I knew I wasn't one hundred per cent yet.

Minus One

Christmas was fast approaching and I looked forward to having no hospital appointments over this two week break. I had other appointments to attend though before this break came. I had regular appointments with the lymphedema clinic, they worked on my chording that once again was healing tight in my arm and restricting movements. I was told to massage the bruised breast area to encourage the hardness from the bruising to dissolve into my body. It was a very strange feeling as the numbness in that area just doesn't feel like part of your body. It was a feeling I had to get used to and I had to make a conscious effort to do this twice daily for five minute sessions.

The next appointment was with the radiologist, in preparation for my radiotherapy after Christmas. He was a doctor full of smiles. He explained that I had to have three tattoos to measure where to blast me! Andrew was quite put out because I'd always told him not to have tattoos and now I was having them! So he asked if I could have a heart, flower and butterfly! To which the doctor said, "You only get those if you go private!" We all had a good laugh. Once again I was finding that laughter was the best medicine!

The tattoos ended up being three tiny black dots, one at either side of my chest and one in the middle. Once that was done I could look forward to Christmas. The church I attend was a wonderful support throughout my experience. Just before Christmas they decided to organise a tree festival and my husband's orchestra would play in a concert to complete the weekend. All the proceeds would go to our local hospital breast care fund. They asked me to say a few words in the concert, so people would know where the money was going. I didn't know if I would be able to do it, but I did and it gave me such a boost that I had come so far. We were able to raise £1,200, it was amazing.

Soon Andrew came down with a nasty bug that left him bed ridden for two days and on Boxing Day my youngest daughter began vomiting and didn't eat anything for five days, which is so unusual for her. In the middle of this my eldest daughter caught the bug as well! I said it would be a miracle if I don't catch this one. Once again I became the antibacterial queen. Well, I believe in miracles and I didn't catch the bug. It was quite amusing that out of everyone, I was the one who didn't catch it. We began to look forward to a holiday when no one was sick. I trusted that this time would come.

It's amazing how a household can change when you are going through this; it began to be normal to hear me shouting, "I've lost my hair!" "Can anyone find my wig?" Andrew would whistle as if he was trying to find a lost dog! I was told that massaging your scalp would help the hair to grow quicker, so my mum would give me a treat and give me a massage. On one occasion when I washed my bra, I was getting ready to go out and realised I had forgotten where I had put my prosthesis! I shouted, "Has anyone seen my boob?" A friend suggested I should have a boob box! I wondered whether I should attach an alarm to it, like you have for missing car keys!

One day, my youngest daughter asked if my boob was going to grow back. I thought this was so sweet but had to tell her I

Minus One

had to have another operation called reconstruction for this to happen. My husband said he wanted to order bigger ones this time! At this time, my nurse suggested we contact an organisation that paid for special days for anyone who had a life threatening illness between the ages of sixteen and forty. We discussed it as a family and the girls wanted to go and see Ant and Dec's *Saturday Night Takeaway* show but sadly they couldn't see another series happening in the foreseeable future. Perhaps it was a good thing because the children were working out all of our embarrassing stories to tell them for the show! For example, when Andrew and I started courting he saw me in town and decided he would come behind me and greet me by grabbing my bottom! Except when I turned around, it wasn't me! He's fortunate he didn't end up with a black eye!

We ended up organising to go and see *The Lion King* West End show and visit Buckingham Palace. It's such a blessing to have organisations like this.

Storms and Blessings

15

It Is Finished

Soon it was time for my radiotherapy sessions to start. The day before my treatment, we went out "as a family" (one of my mum's famous sayings!) for a short bike ride. Yes, I had a bike for Christmas! I did wonder when I would ever ride it, as my last experience was flying over the handle bars in front of a queue of traffic – much to Andrew's amusement and entertainment for the people in the cars! My youngest girl was my coach, she kept saying, "You can do it mum, just stay with me." Well, what an achievement, I didn't fall off and I learnt how to stop! We only went around the local park but it made me feel great. But by the next morning I hurt in places I never knew existed!

I began to get a bit nervous about radio, why? I don't know. The nurses were saying that if you have gone through chemo – radio is nothing. I suppose it's just the unknown again. They were right; there was no need to worry. The radiologists were marvellous and after the first session, I realised there really wasn't anything to be concerned about. It was great to have an experience without any needles involved! I lay on the treatment bench with my arms raised behind my head and was adjusted into positions, like a rag doll. I had four blasts of about thirty seconds each. I found the best lotion to use on my skin was Aloe Vera 99.9%. My skin was able to cope with the radio therapy, with no severe side effects.

I found I felt quite emotional throughout the first week of radiotherapy. The reality of what I was going through hit me. I sat in the waiting area amongst all older people. On one hand, you want someone your own age to walk in but on the other, you don't want anyone else to be going through this. As the sessions went on, I had fifteen in all, I began to feel emotionally stronger. In the last session, I was left alone as usual while they blasted me. The nurses walked out and God's presence came in. It was amazing, it filled the room and I felt complete. I thanked God that my treatment had ended. It is a peculiar feeling to end the treatment, you have to try and get out of the thought process of thinking "what's next?" and realise that it's now ok to think about the future.

On the Sunday after my treatment had ended, I heard a sermon *"It Is Finished."* It was exactly what Helen had written in my jottings journal. The preacher said that this may be the end of your circumstance but the beginning of your destiny. He said that no matter what end you are facing in your life, if we trust in Jesus, He is the beginning and the end, the first and the last and God has given us a destiny.

He said in every day life, we can be overruled by our circumstances, it seems like the end of our dreams, then we stop and give up, but God has our lives in His hands. If we trust in Him, we mustn't stop. We must trust God and believe He will be true to His word. Greater miracles will then be seen. He encouraged the congregation to believe in the best for the future. We all have our God given destiny and He can see beyond our immediate circumstances, and there will be better days ahead. He commented that setbacks can be turned into amazing comebacks. He said that we shouldn't put what we are facing now to become the things that determine the level of our life. We must rise in the face of adversity.

It was such an encouragement to me, to be able to move on from this and trust that this was finished. I still have reconstruction to face and yearly mammograms but I have to trust that God's grace will protect me. As I look back I know that God comforted me, calmed me, secured me and brought me through every situation. After having to face cancer, I now see the world around me through different eyes. I notice how beautiful everything looks on a sunny day; I notice the colours on a blossom tree and the different shades of the sea. I know how special my family and friends are. I have learnt to appreciate life and not take things for granted because it can all change in a second. I have been through storms, I have experienced blessings and now I am heading for my God given destiny.

Storms and Blessings

Epilogue

I have just had the all clear from my first mammogram and scan since my diagnosis. I pray that I will continue to be clear from now on.

My mobile phone has just beeped! It's one of my "bosom buddies" saying "It is a year today that we all met in Ward 2. All wanting a private room! Thank goodness none of us did!" Another text I received was from my great friend, Helen reminding me that this chapter is now finished and it is time to move on and give God the glory.

It's a strange feeling to move on; you have to begin to accept that it's ok to think about the future and make plans. Through all the operations and treatment I found that I could only think and deal with what was happening in the present time and deal with the next stage when it came. Now it is ok to think further than the week I am in. So, it's now time to book a family holiday and send the postcard to my breast care nurse, as promised.

Storms and Blessings